How to Draw
Funky
Animals
and Incredible Creatures

Green Android

Created and produced by Green Android Ltd

Illustrated by Fiona Gowen

Green Android Ltd
49 Beaumont Court
Upper Clapton Road
London E5 8BG
United Kingdom
www.greenandroid.co.uk

ISBN 978-1-909244-02-3

Printed and bound in Dongguan, China, May 2014

Contents

See page 32 for an index of all the animals in this book.

Colourful Fish

There are thousands of types of fish in our rivers and oceans. You can use different styles and colours to make a fun underwater scene.

1 Start with the eye of the fish. Draw a circle with a dot in it.

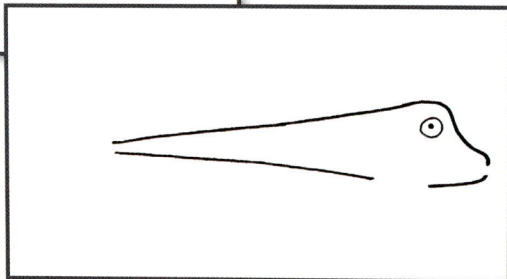

2 Draw a long thin body and a curved face. Leave a gap in the lines for the tail, fins and mouth.

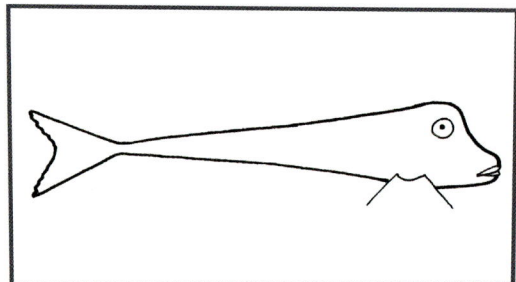

3 Add a tail at the end of the body and a fin underneath. Draw a mouth onto the fish.

4 Draw two thin fins running along the body and large fins above and below the face.

More to Draw
Fish come in different shapes, sizes and patterns.
Try drawing some of these amazing fish.

5 Draw a curved line around the face and a long thin line down the entire length of the body.

Red Gunard

6 Add the final details to the fish. Include small lines on the fins and tail. Add lots of dots over the body.

Flounder

Harlequin Sweetlips

Angel Fish

Sand Eel

Pilot Fish

Sea Dragon

Dogfish

Parrot Fish

Sunfish

Carp

Butterflyfish

Littlehead Porgy

Surgeonfish

Fluttering Beauties

Butterflies and moths have large, often brightly coloured wings. They eat the nectar from flowers and are ideal for adding to drawings of gardens.

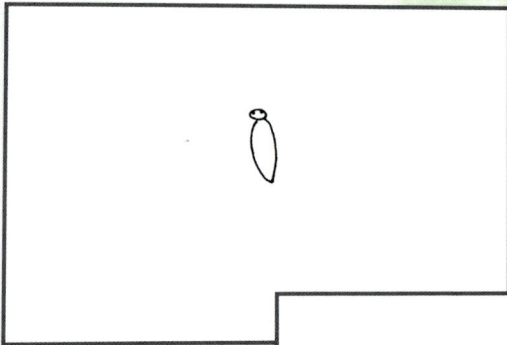

1 Start your drawing with a small circle and an oval.

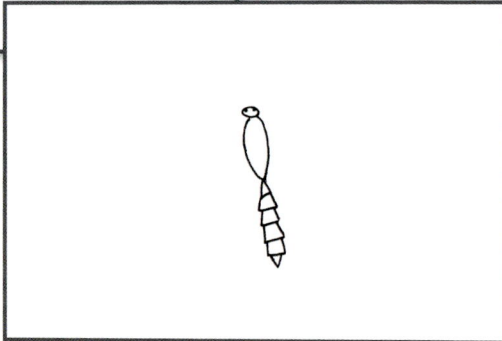

2 Add a section of segments below the oval shape. This will beome the body of your butterfly.

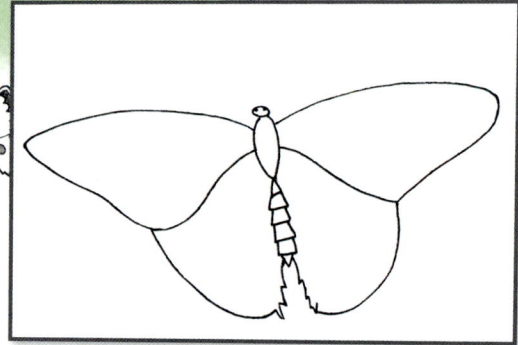

3 Draw some large wings coming out of either side of the butterfly's body.

4 Add some antennae to the head and begin decorating the butterfly's wings.

More to Draw

Butterflies and moths have beautiful patterned wings.
Try drawing some of these pretty examples.

Blue Morpho

Mountain Ringlet

5 Continue to add more details to the wings. Make sure you give the wings symmetrical patterns.

Purple-edged
Copper

Peacock

Monarch

Common Blue

Painted
Lady

Pebble
Prominent

Swallowtail

6 To finish your butterfly drawing add some shading to the patterns on each of the wings.

Ashworth's
Rustic

Cream-bordered
Green Pea

Water Ermine

7

Woodland Wonders

Owls live in trees and only come out during the night. These birds make great additions to drawings of forests and woodlands.

1 Start with a heart–shaped face, two big eyes and a small beak.

2 Draw a big oval shape around the owl's face. Make the bottom of the oval curve inwards for the owl's feet.

3 Add some feet, wings and ears to the owl's feathery body.

Mouse

Hedgehog

4 Add some feathery details around the beak and then begin decorating the owl's face and body.

Great Horned Owl

6 To finish your owl shade the top of its head and areas around its face, ears and body.

5 Shade some of the patterned areas on your owl's body. Also shade some patterns around the face.

Snail

Mole

Tropical Fliers

There are hundreds of tropical birds, including parrots, hornbills, toucans and eagles. These colourful birds are great for forest and jungle drawings.

1 Draw two small eyes and a triangular shaped beak.

2 Add a feathery face and body. Draw two claws onto the body.

3 Draw a branch for the bird to sit on and some long feathers for its tail.

4 Now add plumes around the face. Draw some outlines for the wings.

Some amazing birds live in jungles and rainforests.
Experiment with bright colours for their feathers.

5 Now add some details to the big feathers and texture to the body.

6 Finish the drawing by shading the branch and the bird's wings and tail.

Hawk-head Parrot

Sulphur-crested Cockatoo

Stork-billed Kingfisher

Fischer's Turaco

Hummingbird

White-crowned Hornbill

White-tailed Manakin Bird

Manakin Bird

Six-plumed Bird of Paradise

Graceful Giraffes

Giraffes are the tallest land animals in the world. They live in Africa's savannas, grasslands and woodlands. Draw them near trees as they eat leaves.

1 Draw a box shape for the face and a long line for the neck. Add an eye to the face.

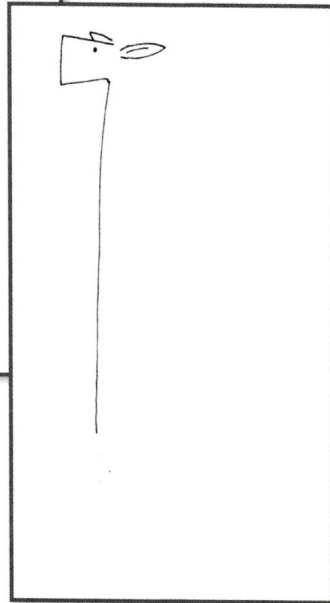

2 Now draw the ears either side of the giraffe's face.

3 Draw a square shape for the snout and two little horns. Draw a line to form the neck and back.

4 Draw another line down the neck. Add the tail, body, legs and feet. Make the giraffe's knees knobbly!

5 Now draw horizontal lines all the way down the back of the giraffe's neck.

6 Finish your giraffe by adding different-sized patches all over the body and neck. Then shade in some detail.

Giraffe

Terrific Tigers

Tigers are the largest of all of the big cats. They are found in South and Southeast Asia and are known for their beautiful stripey fur.

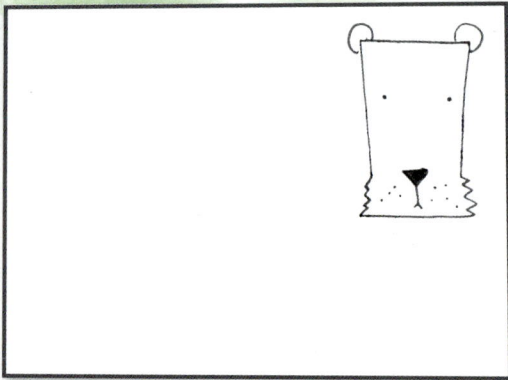

1 Draw a long rectangular face. Add some ears and a triangular nose.

2 Add the body and legs. Remember to add a curved tail. Shade inside the tiger's ears.

3 Now draw stripes over the body and legs. Add some triangle shapes to the face.

4 Shade the triangles on the tiger's face and some of the stripes on the body and legs.

5 Draw small triangles, dots and blocks between some of the stripes on the tiger's body and legs.

6 To finish the drawing you can add even more patterns. Try adding tiny dots along some of the stripes.

Tiger

Incredible Leapers

Frogs and toads are great jumpers and swimmers.
These little creatures can add lovely detail to your
drawings of ponds, rivers and jungle scenes.

1 Start with a big circle for an eye and then draw a line around half of it.

2 Add a curved line for the frog's back. Draw lines for the other eye, mouth and chin.

3 Now add some thin back legs. Draw a small circle at the end of each toe.

4 Draw the front legs bending forwards and add a line for the belly.

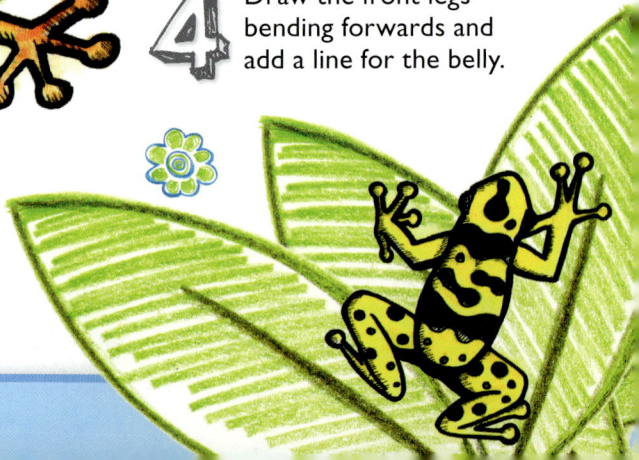

More to Draw

There are many different types of frogs and toads.
Try drawing some of the examples below.

5 Decorate your frog with shapes along the belly and then add a diamond shape in the eye.

6 Use a pencil to shade some areas of the frog, this will help to make your frog drawing look more realistic.

Red-eyed Tree Frog

Golden Poison Frog

Blue Poison-dart Frog

White-lipped Tree Frog

Natterjack Toad

Oriental Fire-bellied Toad

Green Tree Frog

Yellow-banded Poison-dart Frog

Brown Tree Frog

African Giants

These huge animals live in grasslands, forests, deserts and mountains. They live in large family herds so why not make a drawing of a group of elephants?

African Fish-eagle

1 Start your drawing with a triangular ear, an eye and a curved line for the back and top of the head.

2 Add two large legs and a small curved line to make the chin.

3 Draw the large tusk and the curved trunk.

Zebra

Impala

4 Now add the belly and a tail to the elephant.

Elephant

5 Use a pencil to make the outline thicker. Add lines around the trunk and knees.

6 Finally, shade around the belly, legs, ear and trunk to create a realistic look.

How to Draw

Sticky Insects

These strange-looking insects use camouflage to hide from predators. They are great to hide in pictures containing leaves and foliage.

1 Draw a curved shape for wings and a line for the body.

2 Add two thin walking legs and grasping legs in front of the insect's body.

3 Now draw two large eyes and an outline for the insect's face.

4 Draw antennae coming out of the insect's head and add a back set of walking legs.

More to Draw

How many other insects can you think of?
Try drawing some of the unusual ones below.

Lantern Bug

Dock Bug

Grasshopper

Blister Beetle

5 Use a pencil to make the outline thicker. This will help to show the different sections of the insect.

Giraffe-necked weevil

Leaf Insect

Praying Mantis

Tortoise Beetle

6 Finish your drawing by adding shading on the body and details to the wings.

Weevil

Shield Bug

21

How to Draw

Fluffy Friends

It is always fun to draw pictures of your pets and the animals that belong to your friends and family. You can give your drawings to the owners as gifts.

1 Draw a triangle nose and fluffy outline for the dog's head.

2 Continue the fluffy outline up over the dog's nose. Draw the dog's eye underneath the fur.

3 Draw fluffy fur on either side of the nose. Add more fur around the dog's face.

4 Now you can draw the outline of the dog's body. Draw it as a wavy line to show it is furry.

More to Draw
People keep many different types of animals as pets.
Practise copying some of the pets below.

Ferret

Hamster

Rabbit

Pug Dog

5 Add some furry lines across the body of the dog. This will make different sections to shade in.

Gerbil

Cat

Guinea Pig

Old English Sheepdog

6 To finish the drawing, shade some areas darker and add some texture to the fur on the dog's body.

Llama

Chinchilla

Icy Animals

There are different types of penguins that live all over the world, but the most famous are the Emperor penguins that live in the Antarctic.

Gull

1 Draw a large oval outline. Add the head and feet.

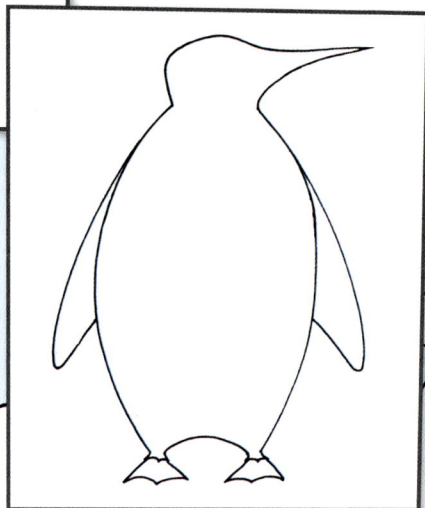

2 Now add wings onto either side of the body and two webbed feet.

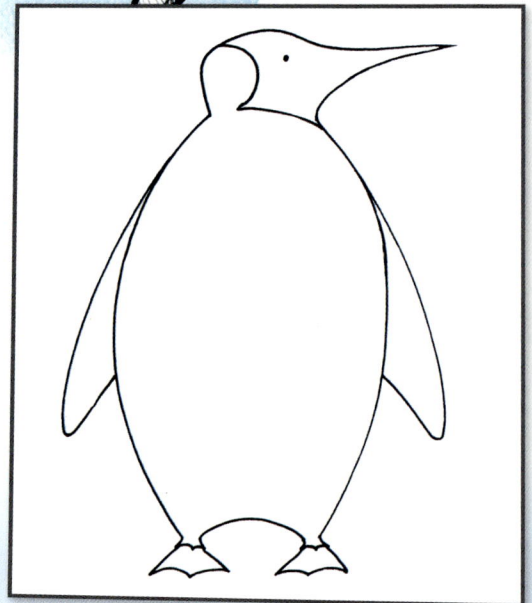

3 Draw this curved shape around the penguin's face and add a small eye.

Polar Bear

Narwhal

Minke Whale

4 Add details to the beak and along the penguin's shoulders and wings.

Emperor Penguin

5 Now you can shade in the face, beak and wings. Don't forget to shade in the penguin's feet.

6 Finish by adding shadows along the outline of the body and under the wings.

Arctic Hare

Walrus

Exotic Lizards

There are thousands of lizards, from tiny geckos to huge Komodo Dragons. Some lizards can change their colour to blend in with their surroundings.

1 Draw lines for the face, the chin and a curved back.

2 Now add the front leg. Make sure the toes are long and pointy.

3 Draw a back leg with the same pointy toes as you drew on the front leg.

4 Draw a curved tail and belly. Add a flap of skin under the chin. This is called a dewlap.

Lizards can be found in places all over the world.
Practise drawing some of these different lizards.

5 Now draw the spiky crest along the iguana's back. Add dots to the face and neck and stripes to the tail.

Green Iguana

6 Finish your iguana by shading stripes down the tail and adding shadows to the underside of the body and neck.

Fire Salamander

Parson's Chameleon

Blue-tailed Skink

Thorny Devil

Madagascan Day Gecko

Flying Dragon

Leopard Gecko

Frill-necked Lizard

Cylindrical Skink

Amazing Swimmers

There are some very fierce-looking animals swimming around our seas, rivers and oceans. Sharks are probably the most feared of all the animals in the ocean.

1 Start the drawing with an long oval shape with a tail at the end.

2 Draw a small black eye and then add some fins along the top and bottom of the body.

3 Now go over the outline again with your pencil to make it really stand out.

More to Draw
There are lots of animals to add to an ocean scene.
Why not try some of these weird creatures?

Female Angler Fish

Jellyfish

4 Add four or five vertical lines to show the gills of the shark.

Hatchetfish

Krill

5 Now you can start adding details to your picture. Draw lots of dots to the front half of the shark's body.

Plankton

Blue-ringed Octopus

Whale Shark

6 To finish your drawing of a shark add lots of bigger dots to the back of the shark's body.

Male Angler Fish

Dragonfish

Fangtooth

How to Draw

Slippery Snakes

Snakes are fun to draw as you can design wild patterns all over their skin. You can add them to drawings of deserts, jungles and woodlands.

Tree Snake

1 Start with a basic outline for the snake. Make the tail into a point.

2 Now add extra lines inside the outline. This is to show the snake's belly.

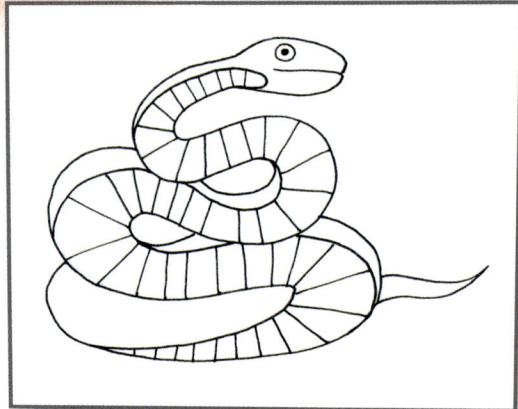

3 Decorate the belly of the snake by adding stripes all the way along.

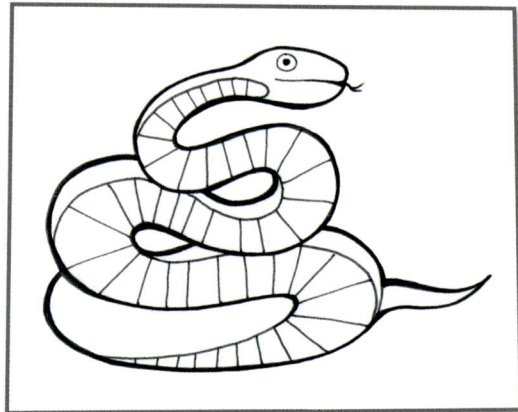

4 Make the outline thicker by drawing over the lines again. Add a thin forked tongue.

Brown Tree Snake

Eastern Tiger Snake

Coral Snake

Amazon
Tree Boa

Paradise
Tree Snake

5 Decorate the rest of the body with thin lines crossing each other to look like scales.

Inland
Taipan

Russell's
viper

6 Finally add shadows underneath the snake's face and body to make your drawing look more realistic.

Animal Index

There are over one hundred different animals in this book. Practice your new-found drawing skills by adding some of them to your drawings.